GW00858787

INCREDIBLE FACTS

Written by Angela Royston
Illustrated by Brian Hoskin

HENDERSON
PUBLISHING PLC
Woodbridge, Suffolk, IP12 1BY England
© 1994 Henderson Publishing plc

BIG NUMBERS

Here is a group of 100 dots:

1000 dots would cover the whole page, but a million dots would more than cover your sitting-room floor.

If a million people joined hands, they could form a chain that stretched from Berlin to Paris.

If this book had a million pages, it would reach from the ground to the top of a 20-storey block of flats.

Even small numbers become large when multiplied by themselves. If you put a 1p coin on the first square of a chess board, 2p on the next square, 4p on the next square and so on, doubling the amount each time, the last square would have over £200,000,000, 000,000,000 on it!

. . . and the pile of coins would reach up into the sky through space, beyond the Moon, even beyond the Sun.

Earth, Sun and Moon

The Sun is a million times bigger than the Earth.

If the Earth was blown up like a balloon to the size of the Sun, then the average 5-year old child would be as tall as the Statue of Liberty.

... and a grapefruit would be no bigger than a grain of salt.

If the Universe shrank so that the Earth was the size of a basketball, the Moon would be as big as a pea. . .

If the Sun and the Earth were both shrunk until the Sun was as big as the Earth, an average family car would fit into a matchbox. . .

. . . and the Sun would be as large as the dome of St Paul's Cathedral.

... even so, in just 6 hours enough sunshine reaches the land to provide the world with all the energy it needs for a year.

Moon days are hotter than the hottest place on Earth, but Moon nights are colder than an Antarctic winter.

Tongues of flame lick out from the Sun into space. Some are as long as the distance between the Earth and the Moon.

The Sun burns 4 million tonnes of hydrogen every second. Luckily there is enough left to keep the Sun shining for another 5000,000,000 years.

The Sun produces enough energy in one second to provide the whole world with electricity for 25 years. Of course, only a fraction of this energy reaches Earth. . .

The rubbish left behind by astronauts will never rot. The footprints left by the astronauts who landed on the Moon over 20 years ago are still there. And if nothing else lands on top of them, they will still be there in a million years time.

There is no wind on the Moon, no rain and no weather. All because there is no air.

There is no sound on the Moon. Meteorites hit the surface in total silence.

The word lunatic comes from the Latin word for the Moon. People used to think that people went mad at full moon.

DISTANCES IN SPACE

Light travels very fast. It could go more than five times around the equator in one second, except that light always travels in straight lines.

Nothing can travel faster than light.

A light-year is the distance light travels in one year - 9,500,000,000,000 kilometres. It takes 8 1/2 minutes for light to reach Earth from the Sun.

It takes 4.3 years for light from the nearest star, Proxima Centauri, to reach us.

Our galaxy, the Milky Way, is probably 100,000 light-years across.

The North Star is 680 light-years away. So the light we see in the sky from this star has taken 680 years to get here. If our telescopes were strong enough to show us what is happening on the North Star we could only see what was happening 680 years ago. So when we look at the stars, we look back in time as well as over vast distances.

If beings on another planet in outer space have strong enough telescopes, they might think we still travel in sailing ships and on horseback, or they might think dinosaurs still roam the land.

THE PLANETS

Venus is the hottest planet. During the day it is eight times as hot as the hottest place on Earth.

Pluto is so cold that if there were any oxygen in the air it would be frozen solid.

Only Earth has the right gases and the right temperature for life to exist.

You would be able to jump about three times as high on Mercury and Mars as you can on Earth.

A day is the time taken for a planet to spin round on its axis. A year is the time taken for it to orbit the Sun. On Venus a day is longer than a year.

A year on Mercury is only eighty eight Earth-days. A 10 year-old Earthling would be over 40 years old on Mercury.

Mercury days are very long. Sunset is over four Earth-weeks after sunrise.

The air on Venus is mainly carbon dioxide. If plants could be grown there, they could eventually turn much of the air into oxygen so animals and humans could live there too. However the process would take over 10,000 years.

If the solar system were shrunk so that Earth was no bigger than a basketball, Mercury would be as large as an orange. You would have to walk 15 minutes to get from the Earth to Mercury and another 10 minutes to get to the Sun. . .

. . . to get to Pluto, however, you would have to drive, nonstop, for over an hour on the motorway.

NEXT JUNCTION
PLUTO

The largest planet is Jupiter and the smallest is Mercury, although distant Pluto may be smaller.

THE STARS

The Sun is one star in the galaxy of stars known as the Milky Way. The Milky Way is a vast whirlpool of stars.

There are more stars in the Universe than there are grains of sand on a beach.

Some stars are bigger than our Sun. Betelgeuse is a supergiant, a million times bigger than our Sun, so big it would swallow Mercury, Venus and Earth.

The nearest star to our Sun is Proxima Centauri. It is so far away, astronomers cannot tell whether it is orbited by any planets.

There are at least 100,000 million other stars in the Milky Way and another 100,000 million galaxies in the Universe.

When a star has burned up all its hydrogen, its core becomes even hotter and it swells up into a huge red giant. Our Sun will be a red giant one day, but not for another 5000 million years.

Some big stars explode. Then they are called supernovae. They may shine as brightly as 100 million of our Suns but they last only for a few hours or days.

Some red giants are as big as our whole solar system. They would reach from the Sun to Pluto.

Some stars are smaller than our Sun. As red giants cool, they change into white dwarfs, smaller perhaps than Earth. White dwarfs are so heavy, one teaspoon would weigh a tonne.

In 1987 astronomers detected the first signals of a supernovae which exploded 170,000 years ago in another galaxy.

If you look at the Moon through a good pair of binoculars, you will see more detail than with the naked eye.

Rockets which launch spacecraft are like huge fireworks. They carry not only their own fuel but also oxygen for burning it.

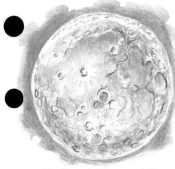

Radio telescopes pick up radio signals rather than light. The dish of the largest one is so big it could hold the whole of Wembley Stadium.

The biggest rocket ever built was as high as a 20-storey building. It was used by the Russians in 1987.

Just over 400 years ago the Roman Catholic church banished anyone who believed that the Earth orbited the Sun. They insisted that the Earth was at the centre of the Universe.

The first satellite launched into orbit around the Earth was *Sputnik 1*. It was about the size of a large beach ball.

Spacemen are weightless. With no gravity to keep their feet on the floor, they simply float around. They have to be very tidy, because anything they drop floats about.

Russian astronauts who stayed in space for a year spent much of the time exercising on a machine to avoid the bad effects of weightlessness. They had to be strapped to the machine, of course.

The first person to play golf on the Moon was Alan Shepherd. He whacked a piece of Moon rock with a soil-sample scoop. Had he had a golf ball and club he could have covered five holes in a single shot.

Pioneer 10 was launched in 1972. It carries coded pictures and information about Earth. It is on its way to a star cluster called M13, but it is not expected to arrive for another 25,000 years.

Being weightless may be fun for a short time, but after a while your muscles begin to shrink and your bones become brittle.

SPACE JUNK

In 1800 the Celestial Police were formed. Their mission was to find a planet between Mars and Jupiter. This band of twenty four astronomers found not just one planet, but a belt of space junk - pieces of rock left over when the planets formed. They are called asteroids and over 2000 have now been identified.

A million tonnes of meteorites fall on Earth every year. Most are no bigger than specks of dust. Shake your coat - it's probably covered in fine cosmic dust.

A shooting star is not a star but a meteoroid burning up in the Earth's atmosphere.

Meteoroids which are too large to burn up hit the ground. Then they are called meteorites.

A huge meteorite which hit the Earth 64 million years ago was probably responsible for the sudden disappearance of the dinosaurs.

The Fragile Crust

If the Earth were the size of a basketball, the solid land we call the Earth's crust would be no thicker than a grape skin.

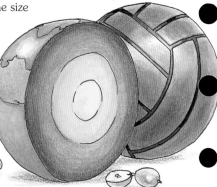

Volcanoes and Earthquakes

Over a million earthquakes shake the land each year, but most of them are too slight for us to notice. Movements in the Earth's crust cause earthquakes.

At one time the icy continent of Antarctica was on the equator.

The Greeks thought that the wrestling of huge, subterranean giants caused earthquakes. The Algonquin Indians thought that a giant tortoise carried the Earth on its back. When the tortoise shuffled its feet, the Earth shook.

In 1976 about 300,000 people were killed when an earthquake struck Tangshan in China. The force produced by the earthquake was 5000 times greater than that of the atom bomb which was dropped on Hiroshima, Japan, during the Second World War. This bomb was so terrible the Japanese immediately surrendered.

In 1883 a volcano on the island of Krakatoa erupted. The bang was so loud it was heard in Australia - over 5000 kilometres away.

Tsunamis (sometimes called tidal waves) are caused by earthquakes in the land below the sea. One of the biggest hit the coast of Siberia in 1737. It was as high as a 20-storey building.

In 1963 the island of Surtsey suddenly appeared in the sea near Iceland. It was made by the cooling lava of an underwater volcano.

Oceans

The world's highest mountain is under the sea. Its tip is Mauna Kea on the island of Hawaii. Its base is 9000 metres under the sea.

The deepest place in the oceans is the bottom of the Marianas Trench, 11,022 metres below the surface of the Pacific Ocean. If you sank Mount Everest in the Marianas Trench and dropped Mount Kosciusko (the highest mountain in Australia) on top of it, only 54 metres of land would show above water.

There is enough salt in the sea to cover all the land with a layer half the height of the Eiffel Tower.

The sea also contains gold, but, unfortunately, not as much as it does salt. You would have to sift through a million litres of sea water just to get 4 grams of gold!

Mountains and Caves

Mount Everest, the world's highest mountain, is as tall as a 2000-storey skyscraper.

Although Mount Kenya is on the Equator, its top is as cold as the Arctic. The temperature drops about 1 degree for every 100 metres you climb, so if you are mountain climbing - take warm clothes with you.

Mount Everest is getting higher. As India pushes into the rest of Asia, the Himalayas continue to be pushed up.

The Sarawak Chamber in Malaysia is the largest cave in the world. It is as large as three football pitches and higher than Nelson's Column in Trafalgar Square, London.

Beneath the ground near Krakow in Poland is an underground 'city' carved out of salt. The church was carved out over 300 years ago by miners. More recently, a hospital, snack bar, tennis court and dance floor have been carved out too.

Rivers, Lakes and Waterfalls

The Amazon in South America is the widest river in the world. If London were on one bank, Paris would be on the other bank.

The mighty Amazon contains more water than any other river. In fact it contains a fifth of all the world's river water.

Waterfalls wear away the rocks over which they flow. The Victoria Falls in Zimbabwe has moved 130 kilometres back up the Zambezi River since it started flowing a few thousand years ago.

The winter of 1848 was so cold that the Niagara Falls, on the border of Canada and the United States, froze solid.

Lake Superior in North America is the largest freshwater lake in the world. It is twice as big as the country of Switzerland.

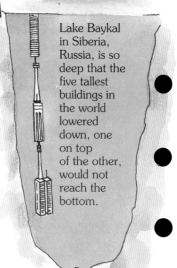

Lake Baykal in Siberia, Russia, is so deep that the five tallest buildings in the world lowered down, one on top of the other, would not reach the bottom.

Deserts

The world's largest desert, the Sahara, is as big as the United States of America and nearly as big as the whole of Europe.

The Atacama desert in Chile, South America, is the driest place in the world. One part got no rain at all for 400 years.

Deserts are dry, rocky or sandy places, with scarcely a plant to be seen. But when it does rain a mass of flowers burst into bloom. Their seeds may have been lying in the soil for 20 years waiting for water.

Rock paintings in Algeria show that elephants and rhinos once roamed the Sahara - before it became a desert.

The Sahara is blistering hot during the day, but very cold at night.

Many desert animals burrow underground to get away from the extreme heat and cold. In Coober Pedy in Australia, people do the same. Houses, hotels, bars and leisure halls are built underground. The Aborigines call the town 'kupa pitt', which means 'white man in a hole'.

Ice and Snow

Nine-tenths of all the world's ice lies on top of Antarctica. The ice is so heavy that it pushes the land down below the level of the sea.

If all this ice melted, the oceans would rise by over 60 metres. Seaside towns and cities would be flooded as would most of Holland, Belgium and Bangladesh.

As a glacier reaches the sea, huge chunks of ice break off and float away as icebergs. The biggest iceberg ever seen was as large as the country of Belgium. It was spotted off Antarctica in 1956.

Glaciers are rivers of ice which move very slowly. A snowflake which falls in the middle of Greenland would take 3000 years to reach the sea.

During the summer at the Poles, the Sun never sets. During the winter, it never rises.

Storms and Weather

The strongest winds are whipped up by tornadoes. These whirling funnels of air move slowly over the ground, sucking trees, roofs and animals into the air. In 1980 twelve children in China were sucked up by a tornado and carried 20 kilometres before landing, unhurt, on a sand dune.

There is no wind at the centre of a hurricane. It is called the eye of the storm. The winds blow around the eye and can last for several days.

It never actually rains cats and dogs, but it has occasionally rained fish, or frogs. Scientists think that they may have been sucked up by mini tornadoes.

The least windy part of the world is a band of ocean just north and south of the tropics. They are called the 'horse latitudes' because, when a sailing ship became becalmed and food and drink ran short, any horses on board were the first to be thrown overboard.

The hottest place in the world is Al'Aziziyah in Libya. The temperature here has reached a sizzling 58 degrees Centigrade, only a little hotter than Death Valley in California.

Hailstones as big as melons fell on Gopalganj in Bangladesh in 1986. They killed 92 people!

On the south coast of Australia, the temperature can drop by up to 20 degrees Centigrade in a few minutes. The Southerly Buster is a wind which blows off the ocean from Antarctica, plunging sunbathers straight into winter temperatures.

Tutunendo in Colombia, South America, is the wettest place in the world. If none of the rain drained away, even 4-storey buildings would be under water at the end of a year.

PREHISTORIC TIMES

Evolving World

The Earth formed 4600 million years ago. If the time since then and now were reduced to one year, beginning on January 1st, then:

the land was bare and lifeless until November 29th, ...

the dinosaurs roamed the Earth for just over 13 days, from 6 pm on December 12th until 12 minutes past 7 pm on December 25th, and ...

> The Great Deluge would have lasted for just over 6 minutes on February 16th, ...

> Jesus Christ was born just 14 seconds ago.

the first simple forms of life appeared in the sea at the end of March, ...

The largest insects that have ever lived were giant dragonflies. Their wings were as wide as a seagull's. They became extinct just before the dinosaurs appeared.

Quetzalcoatlus was a huge flying reptile, about the same size as a Spitfire fighter plane from World War II.

As the last ice age ended, people were living in caves and large, hairy mammoths roamed southern Europe. We know this because people drew pictures of them on the walls of their caves!

Eohippus, the ancient ancestor of today's horses, was no bigger than a tabby cat.

Mammoth's tusks were so long that if a mammoth looked through your open sitting room window, its tusks would touch the opposite wall.

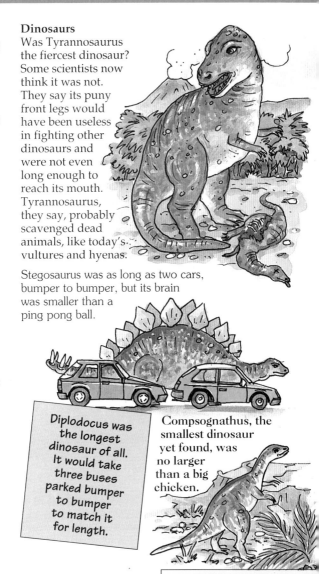

Dinosaurs

Was Tyrannosaurus the fiercest dinosaur? Some scientists now think it was not. They say its puny front legs would have been useless in fighting other dinosaurs and were not even long enough to reach its mouth. Tyrannosaurus, they say, probably scavenged dead animals, like today's vultures and hyenas.

Stegosaurus was as long as two cars, bumper to bumper, but its brain was smaller than a ping pong ball.

Diplodocus was the longest dinosaur of all. It would take three buses parked bumper to bumper to match it for length.

Compsognathus, the smallest dinosaur yet found, was no larger than a big chicken.

Dinosaurs became extinct very suddenly. Scientists now think that a huge meteor or comet hit the Earth, sending up clouds of dust which blotted out the Sun. The weather would have become very cold, killing off the dinosaurs.

A huge crater, as large as Belgium, has been detected under the Gulf of Mexico and dates from the time the dinosaurs died out. If an equally large meteor fell today on Mexico, the force of the impact would shake buildings in London.

Dinosaur eggs were about as big as a rugby ball. If the mother dinosaur had sat on them (like a bird on a nest) she would have smashed them. Instead she probably buried them in a heap of rotting leaves.

The skulls of some dinosaurs were as thick as two bricks. They probably used to bang heads to see who was strongest!

Strange Facts

Squirrels use their tails like parachutes. They have been seen falling from trees as high as a 50-storey building without hurting themselves.

Sloths spend almost all their lives hanging upside-down from the branch of a tree. They move very slowly. A sloth in a hurry still takes 15 seconds to cover a metre.

If sloths are the laziest animals, swifts may be the most active. They can fly non-stop for years at a time. They eat, drink and even sleep in the air. But they have to land to hatch their eggs.

Dolphins have been known to rescue drowning swimmers by nudging them to the surface with their snouts and even flicking them onto the shore.

Archer fish catch their prey by spitting at them. From the surface of the pond, they shoot down insects clinging to overhanging leaves.

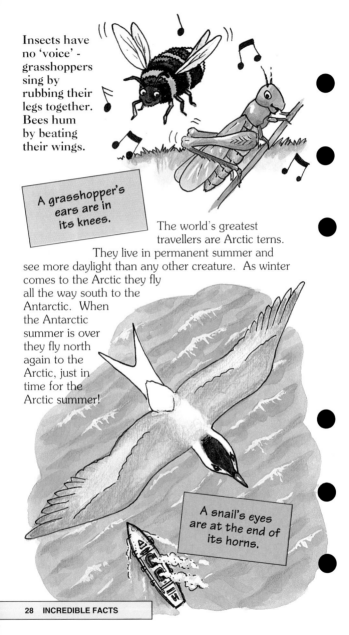

Insects have no 'voice' - grasshoppers sing by rubbing their legs together. Bees hum by beating their wings.

A grasshopper's ears are in its knees.

The world's greatest travellers are Arctic terns. They live in permanent summer and see more daylight than any other creature. As winter comes to the Arctic they fly all the way south to the Antarctic. When the Antarctic summer is over they fly north again to the Arctic, just in time for the Arctic summer!

A snail's eyes are at the end of its horns.

Many oak trees are 200-400 years old. They started growing when Elizabeth I was queen of England and Shakespeare was writing his plays. But they are no more than saplings compared to. . .

. . . the world's oldest tree which is 4600 years old. A bristle-cone pine grows in Arizona, USA. It started growing when the pyramids were being built in Ancient Egypt. It was 2000 years old when the Roman Empire was at its height.

Plovers are the only animals that are not afraid of a crocodile's jaws. They hop into the crocodile's mouth and peck off the bits of food stuck between its teeth.

Snakes can open their mouths very wide. A reticulated python once managed to swallow a bear.

A starfish looks pretty but its feeding habits are disgusting! It wraps its arms around the tightly-closed shell of an oyster or mussel and prises it open. Then it brings its stomach out through its mouth and pushes it, inside out, into the shell. The stomach then starts to digest the meal.

Beavers' front teeth are so sharp that early people used them as knives.

A thread of a spider's web is as strong as steel of the same thickness.

Largest and Smallest

The largest animal that has ever lived is the Blue whale. If one went for a swim in your local public

pool, it would fill it with only 10 metres to spare each end.

Blue whales feed on some of the world's smallest animals - plankton. They swallow up to a tonne of these microscopic animals at each meal.

A Californian giant sequoia known as 'General Sherman' is the most massive tree in the world. It is not as tall as some of the Australian eucalyptus trees but its trunk is 8 metres across, wider than the average house.

Australian eucalyptus trees are the world's tallest trees. They can grow higher than St Paul's Cathedral in London.

The world's biggest nut is the fruit of the coco-de-mer. Each one may weigh as much as 150 apples.

Millipedes have the most legs - about 700.

One rainforest tree may be home to 800 different kinds of insects.

Elephants are really heavy. It would take over 70 average-sized men to weigh as much as an elephant.

An area of rainforest the size of a football pitch is being cut down every second.

Grizzly bears are bigger and heavier than even the biggest wrestlers. Four wrestlers weighed together might still be lighter than a Grizzly.

Animal Families

Male bowerbirds build elaborate structures of twigs and leaves which can be almost as high as a room - just to attract a mate. But once he has a mate, he doesn't lift a claw or a beak to help build the actual nest!

An Emperor penguin father, on the other hand, spends the coldest Antarctic months holding a fertilised egg on his feet and keeping it warm. When the egg hatches he feeds it with the last remaining food from his stomach.

A female Green turtle lays about 1800 eggs during her life, but of these about 1400 don't hatch and 370 are killed by predators soon after birth. Of the remaining 30, only 3 grow up to mate and produce eggs themselves.

Even if an average pet cat is allowed to have only one litter, that one litter may give rise to more than 20,000 cats in just two years.

The fastest breeder is a bacteria which lives in the human gut. In the right conditions it splits in two every 15 minutes, producing 40,000,000,000, 000,000,000,000, 000,000 more bacteria in just 24 hours.

Kangaroos can be as large as people but a newborn kangaroo baby (called a joey) is only 1 centimetre long. This tiny creature has to find its own way through its mother's fur to her pouch. Once here it settles down to feed on her milk and grow bigger.

Opossums and wombats have backwards-facing pouches so their babies do not get showered with earth when the mothers burrow underground.

Animal Olympics

Frogs can jump over 100 times their own length. If you could jump as well as a frog, you could leap over one football pitch and land on the halfway line of a second.

If the world's fastest sprinter ran against a jackrabbit in the 100 metres, the sprinter would have reached only halfway when the jackrabbit crossed the finishing line.

Fleas, however, are the jumping champions. If you could jump as well as a flea, you could jump the length of four football pitches laid end to end and as high as a 60-storey building.

A car would have to break the speed limit to catch up with a cheetah on the motorway.

Cheetahs are the fastest runners, but only over short distances. A prong-horned antelope can keep going for much longer. If the cheetah hadn't caught it in the first 10 seconds, the antelope would almost certainly get away.

Professional divers in Acapulco, Mexico, dive into the sea off cliffs as high as an 11-storey building. This is nothing compared to a sperm whale which can dive as deep as a kilometre - three times as deep as the Eiffel Tower is high.

The fastest animal of all is the spine-tailed swift from Asia. It is claimed that they can fly as fast as the top speed of a racing car.

An ant can lift a weight 50 times heavier than itself. Just suppose you could do the same!

An ant can drag a twig 300 times as heavy as itself. If ants were as big as people, just two of them could drag a loaded articulated truck off the road!

Human Body
Blinking is your fastest action and you can do it up to 200 times a minute. Hummingbirds, however, beat their wings over 20 times as fast.

It is almost impossible not to blink for as long as a minute.

The Romans despised long hair and beards. They opened the first barber's shop nearly 1500 years ago.

Solid food stays in your stomach about 3 hours, but it takes another 20 hours to pass right through your body.

Your stomach holds about a litre of mushed-up food. Compare this to a cow's stomach which can hold 180 times as much - over 20 buckets of food. No wonder cows spend all day munching.

It takes over twice as many muscles to frown as it does to smile. Keep smiling!

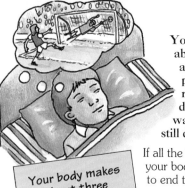

You usually have about five dreams a night, but you probably only remember a dream if you wake up while still dreaming.

If all the blood vessels in your body were laid end to end they would stretch over twice around the Equator.

Your lungs consist of millions of tiny balloons of air. If each balloon was opened up and flattened out they would cover an area as big as a tennis court.

Your body makes about three mugfulls of spit a day. Stop swallowing and within a minute your mouth will be full of spit.

Your lungs hold about 3 litres of air. As much as in a large empty milk container.

The air you breathe has probably already been breathed in and out several times before. It is the same air as the dinosaurs breathed.

By the time you are 10 years old, your heart will have beaten nearly 400,000,000 times.

When you sneeze, air rushes through your nose faster than a car on the motorway.

No other animal apart from humans laugh.

Each red blood cell lives only for one or two months. Your body manufactures nearly 2 million new red blood cells every second.

A pinprick of blood contains over 5 million cells. Most of these are red cells which makes your blood look red.

Your blood travels all around your body more than once every minute. When you are running fast, your blood flows faster too - up to five times around your body every minute.

Brain cells are so small over 300 would fit onto this full stop.

Nerves carry messages to and from the brain so fast they would reach from one end of a football pitch to the other in less than a second.

You are about 1 centimetre smaller when you go to bed than when you woke up. During the day the weight of your head squashes the soft cartilage between the bones of your spine. It bounces back at night.

The longest bones in your body are the upper thigh bones. The smallest bones are the tiny ones in your ears called the stirrup.

Your hair and nails are made of the same stuff as horns and claws.

If you want to live to be very old, move to the Caucasus Mountains between the Black Sea and the Caspian Sea. Many people here live to be over 110 years old.

Your hair grows just over 1 centimetre a month. Since each hair only grows for about 6 years before falling out, most people cannot grow their hair longer than 70-80 centimetres.

Travel

Hot air balloons were invented before aeroplanes. The first passengers to fly in a hot air balloon were a duck, a sheep and a cockerel.

The world's fastest plane is powered by rockets. It could cover the distance between London and New York in 46 minutes (not counting take-off and landing).

The fastest plane can go seven times as fast as the fastest car which can go nearly twice as fast as the fastest boat.

Concorde is the fastest passenger plane. It flies twice as fast as the speed of sound and can fly from New York to London in less than 3 hours.

The fastest ships skim across the surface of the water. A hydroplane called *Spirit of Australia*, reached 556 kilometres/hour. At that speed, it could cross the English Channel in less than 7 minutes.

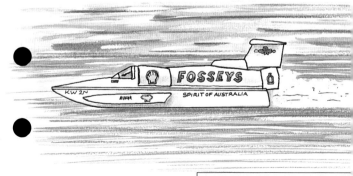

The biggest ships in the world are oil tankers. Many are so long you could mark out four football pitches along the deck and still have room to spare. One ship could carry enough petrol to fill the tanks of over 4 million cars.

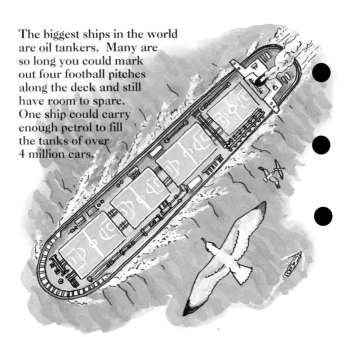

The Volkswagen Beetle is the most popular car ever made. Over 21 million have been bought since 1938.

The longest train journey you can make without changing trains is from Moscow in Russia to Nakhodka on the edge of the Pacific Ocean. This journey on the Trans-Siberian railway takes 8 days.

Communications

Newspapers have always irritated powerful people. The very first one published in Boston over 300 years ago was instantly banned because it included stories of the French King Louis XIV's love affairs with his mistresses.

A Japanese company has made a silicon chip which can store all the words in a 160-page book on an area no larger than your fingernail.

Inventions and Discoveries

The world's most revolutionary invention was the wheel!

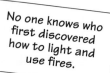

The Chinese discovered that silk produced by the silk worm can be woven into cloth. They kept the discovery secret for hundreds of years so all silk was brought thousands of miles overland from China to Europe.

No one knows who first discovered how to light and use fires.

A Greek inventor called Hero invented many machines including a slot machine which dispensed holy water and a steam engine. It was not until over a thousand years later that steam engines were developed which transformed factories and transport.

When chocolate was first brought to Europe from South America it was used to flavour meat. Then someone had the bright idea of adding sugar to it.

Green Facts
The average American family uses the equivalent of eight baths of water a day.

Brushing your teeth with the tap running uses nearly 10 litres of water.

Cars waste three quarters of the energy available in petrol.

Every year most families throw away the equivalent of four trees in paper.

A quarter of the world's population use four times as much of the Earth's resources as the other three-quarters. Where does that quarter live? - in Europe, North America and Australasia.

Buildings and Structures

The world's highest bridge crosses the Royal Gorge in Colorado, USA. The drop from the bridge is greater than that from the top of the Eiffel Tower.

The Great Pyramid is the biggest stone building in the world. It was built 4000 years ago and is large enough to fit in three buildings the size of St Paul's Cathedral in London.

The Pentagon, the US government building in Washington, is so big you could fit St Peter's in Rome, the Great Pyramid, the Colosseum in Rome and Stonehenge into the same area, at the same time.

The Great Wall of China, built over 2000 years ago, is the only manmade structure which can be seen from the Moon.

Start with any number you like, say 127, and multiply it by 9. Add the digits of the answer (1143) together. The answer is always 9! If the answer is more than 10, add the digits again. The final answer will always be 9.

Maths and Science
You cannot fold a sheet of paper in half more than seven times. And it's no help to start with a larger sheet. Try it.

Every snowflake is different.

Nothing can travel faster than light. As something gets close to the speed of light, it gets heavier and heavier and time slows down. If a spaceship travelled at nearly the speed of light, hundreds of Earth years may have passed before the astronauts returned in their own lifetime.

Even very solid objects consist mostly of space - the space between the electrons and nucleus in each atom. The structure of an atom is similar to that of the Sun and planets. Electrons spin around a central nucleus.

If a single hair of your head and mine were negatively charged with electricity and we stood within touching distance, we would both be thrown backwards across the room.

Animals can see colours that we cannot. What to us may be a plain yellow flower is patterned with ultraviolet to a bee.
Bats and whales produce ultrasonic squeaks that we cannot hear without a special machine.

Although we cannot hear it, ultrasonic noise can make us ill. Some heavy machinery and the air intake on a jet engine produce ultrasonic noise that can make workers feel sick and dizzy.

If infinity exists it must be a dull place. It is where all parallel lines meet and the counting numbers end. It is where 'for ever' stops.

White light is actually made up of all the colours of the rainbow combined together. We only see a rainbow when light at a certain angle has been broken down into its separate colours.